YOUR KNOWLEDGE HAS VALUE

Bibliographic information published by the German National Library:

The German National Library lists this publication in the National Bibliography; detailed bibliographic data are available on the Internet at http://dnb.dnb.de .

Imprint:

Copyright © 2009 GRIN Verlag, Open Publishing GmbH
Print and binding: Books on Demand GmbH, Norderstedt Germany
ISBN: 9783656952381

This book at GRIN:

http://www.grin.com/en/e-book/298849/guilt-in-ian-mcewan-s-atonement-and-joe-wright-s-film-adaptation

Carmen Odimba

Guilt in Ian McEwan's "Atonement" and Joe Wright's film adaptation

GRIN Publishing

GRIN - Your knowledge has value

Since its foundation in 1998, GRIN has specialized in publishing academic texts by students, college teachers and other academics as e-book and printed book. The website www.grin.com is an ideal platform for presenting term papers, final papers, scientific essays, dissertations and specialist books.

Visit us on the internet:

http://www.grin.com/

http://www.facebook.com/grincom

http://www.twitter.com/grin_com

Johannes Gutenberg-Universität Mainz
Fachbereich Translations-, Sprach- und Kulturwissenschaft
in Germersheim

Course: Transferring & Translating Media (Novels to Film):
Ian McEwan's *Atonement*

Paper: **Guilt in Ian McEwan's *Atonement* and
Joe Wright's film adaptation**

Student: Carmen Odimba

Scheduled for : Summer term 2009

CONTENTS

1. Introduction

Atonement, the novel by Ian McEwan published in 2001, is qualified by many critics as a "wartime love story". It is an interpretation that suits the glamorous criteria needed by the public and provided by the media nowadays. But this interpretation focuses only on Cecilia and Robbie, as they are considered to be the victims in the story and therefore forgets the important part that Briony or her writing process play in the novel and Joe Wright's film.

A complete reading of *Atonement* should include a study of the title and its implications in the story. We will start by analyzing the meaning of the word "atonement". The choice of this title has a special significance for the whole novel and should lead us readers and spectators to understand its message – to know whether the spirit of the novel has been respected by the film maker is a question to which we will also answer briefly.

The tragic event that happened in Part One of the novel would never have taken place if the social environment had been more opened. With other codifications, more courage and less things left unsaid, the story would have been different. We will examine some of the taboos that played an important role in the shaping of *Atonement*'s characters.

The notion of guilt is very present in the novel, thus it will be, in relation to atonement, the central focus of this paper. We will consider the main characters, i.e. Briony, Robbie, Cecilia, Lola and Paul Marshall and try to evaluate the degree to which each one of them is guilty, feels guilty and is willing to atone for his sins.

The last part of the paper will be essentially dedicated to the film, to Joe Wright's interpretation of the concepts we named above. Considering our paper's subject, was it a good or a bad adaptation?

2. What is atonement ?

The word *atonement* was invented in the sixteenth century by the reformer William Tyndale who recognized that there was no English equivalent for the biblical Hebraic concept.

2.1. A Judaic and Christian doctrine based on culpability

Christianity finds its roots in the Judaic doctrine and Christians were issued from the Jewish people. Therefore, both doctrines have common elements such as the belief in the necessity of atonement.

In Rabbinic Judaism, atonement is achieved through several different combinations of repentance, Temple service, confession, restitution, the occurrence of Yom Kippur, tribulations, the carrying out of a sentence of corporal or capital punishment imposed by an ordained court (nowadays not anymore) and the experience of dying.
Which of these are required varies according to the severity of the sin and the implication into its performing (whether it was done willingly or not).

According to the Bible, atonement is the action of making amends for an injury or wrong, so that mankind and God can be reconciled.
Sin makes impure and provokes a sanction that is inevitably death, the separation from God.

> Genesis 2:17
> 17 but of the tree of the knowledge of good and evil, thou shalt not eat of it. For in the day that thou eatest thereof, thou shalt surely die.

> Romans 5:12
> 12 Therefore, as by one man sin entered into the world, and death by sin, so death passed onto all men, for all have sinned.

> Romans 6:23
> 23 For the wages of sin is death, but the gift of God is eternal life through Jesus Christ our Lord.

And yet Christ has atoned for all sins by taking on the responsibility personally and enduring the punishment for all mankind. The sin is atoned, i.e. forgiven, and mankind is freed from evil and from a fair sentence.

The Bible constantly warns against sin and sinful behavior, thus creating a feeling of guilt and the necessity to atone for every mistake.

> Exodus 29:36
> 36And thou shalt offer every day a bullock for a sin offering for atonement; and thou shalt cleanse the altar when thou hast made an atonement for it, and thou shalt anoint it to sanctify it.

> Exodus 29:37
> 37Seven days thou shalt make an atonement for the altar and sanctify it; and it shall be an altar most holy. Whatsoever toucheth

the altar shall be holy.

2.2.   Guilt and atonement in psychology

We have just acknowledged that guilt and atonement are concepts so important to the human being that they are evoked in the Bible, one of the oldest texts that exist.
Pruyser suggests that the satisfactory theory, that sees the death of Christ as being offered to provide satisfaction to assuage God's righteous anger at humanity's rebellion, and to enable him to be merciful, has a particular resonance for those who are easily overwhelmed by their feelings of guilt. Such people are likely to be dominated by their super-ego, an almost tyrannical entity. For them, the satisfaction theory brings the assurance that the price of guilt has been paid, releasing the fullness of God's forgiveness for wrongdoing.

Modern psychology draws a very fine line between guilt and atonement. Although guilt traditionally (Jewish, Catholic, Puritan) have a negative connotation, psychologists keep finding evidence of its usefulness. Allan Carr sees atonement as a positive process.

> Atonement, too, has its benefits. When we atone for transgressions we reduce our feelings of guilt and may also elicit forgiveness from those against whom we have transgressed. Atonement and repentance may also improve psychological and physical well-being. However, there are barriers to atonement. Atonement entails acknowledging personal responsibility for wrongdoing, experiencing the feelings of guilt and shame that go with this acknowledgement, and accepting the punishment associated with the transgression [...] this may involve legal penalties such as imprisonment. (Carr 255)

The following passage will help us a lot in the analysis of Briony's and other characters's attempts of atonement in Chapter 4.

> Both forgiveness and atonement require us to put pride aside and be humble. Humility involves seeing oneself as no better or no worse than others. Both forgiveness and atonement require us to empathise with the other person's position (be they transgressor or victim) and understand how the situation looks from their perspective. Setting pride aside, humility and empathy – all extremely challenging processes since they render us vulnerable to attack – are major obstacles to engaging in forgiveness or atonement. (Carr 255)

Too little guilt can be catastrophic, like for sociopaths who feel no remorse, but also as early as for kindergartners who smack other children and steal their toys.
According to Grazyna Kochanska, children generally start to feel guilt in their second year of life. One of her studies showed that 2-year-old children that experienced guilt have less behavioral problems over the next five years. Some of these children later become more guilt-prone thanks to parents and other early influences.

Kant split the human person into two entities - body and soul, act and intention, objective and subjective, the world 'out there' and the world 'in here'. All that matters morally, is what happens 'in here', in the soul. But a culture that confines morality to the mind is one that lacks an adequate defense against harmful behavior: passivity or indifference, even without any bad intention, in a war context, for example, can be considered as condemnable.

3. Social taboos in the 1930s England

Feelings like remorse, guilt and shame often come from the fact of having done or doing something that is not aloud, considered as evil or that one should not mention in public. The environment in which the characters of *Atonement* evolve is suffocating because of left unsaid things. In this section, we will focus on the social taboos that influenced Cecilia and Briony's education.

3.1. Women start to smoke in public

Cecilia lighting a cigarette on the steps in part 1 of the novel is not the innocent scene that it seems to be. In the 1930s, women smoking in public was a new fashion that was not appreciated by everyone. This habit will become more and more common during the wartime.

Cecilia lights a cigarette during her father's absence, which is the only kind of rebellion she can afford. Throughout the book, this should be perceived as the sign of torment and this symbol is repeated in the film: the scene in the steps, the cigarette she smokes with Robbie outside (also provocative in a sensual way), the cigarette smoked alone on the porch outside while waiting for Robbie. Cecilia never looses her composure throughout the whole film, except while she read Robbie's note handed by Briony and in the library, but the lighting of a cigarette always signals impatience.

3.2. Family collapse

> [...] We can't go home anyway...' He paused to gather his courage. 'It's a divorce!'
> Pierrot and Lola froze. The word had never been used in front of the children, and never uttered by them. The soft consonants suggested an unthinkable obscenity, the sibilant ending whispered the family's shame. (McEwan 57)

In a society based on Christian values, divorce, still very often considered as a shame or crime, was a reality that was hidden to the children.

After this passage, Lola will ask Paul not to repeat anything of what he has read in the newspapers about their parents to her younger brothers.

Mrs Tallis turns a blind eye to Mr Tallis's very busy work schedule, although it is very probable that he in fact has a mistress with whom he spends more and more time. Does Mrs Tallis not know what is going on? We suspect that she does but refuses to risk to break the family's image by a fight or to loose the lifestyle she is used to if she were to divorce. She might also do this for the love of her children or because she loves Mr Tallis enough to forgive him. We should also not forget that Mrs Tallis has a fragile health condition and that she is therefore very likely to avoid any kind of unnecessary stress.

3.3. Sexuality

Preadolescents nowadays tend to know much or to be already interested by sexuality. They know that boys were not born in cabbages and that girls were not born in roses. This early awareness of their own body can be noticed in the dressing habits or the behavior of these young people. In 1998, Sean Stewart became the youngest father in the United Kingdom; he was only twelve years old. He was eleven as his four-year older girlfriend became pregnant, which is of course terribly early as he was not even a preadolescent yet, but a child himself. Paradoxically, such events are caused by the same fact that produced Briony's ignorance: the lack of sexual education.

A thirteen-year old girl in the 1930s in England did not know much about the mechanisms of love and desire. Although Briony is perceived by the reader and the spectator as extremely silly and even criminal (she "separated" two lovers), she is only the product of her education, an education made of fairy tales and princesses, without nudity or any reference to her anatomy. Although "it [is] right [and] essential, for her to know everything" (McEwan 113), she is not prepared to it. Briony therefore perceives an intensely erotic scene by the fountain as something strange and the scene in the library as an attack on the person of Cecilia.
According to Briony's education, sexuality, whatever it might be, is something that should not happen before or outside of marriage or, for Briony herself, that should better not happen at all: In Part One, chapter One, she thinks "A good wedding was an unacknowledged representation of the as yet unthinkable – sexual bliss"(McEwan 9).

Even if Briony saw things that she could not understand in the library or by the fountain, a little bit of dialogue could have avoided the following misunderstanding. Cecilia could have tried to explain to Briony that what she has seen is actually something normal and that it happens when two people love each other. She could have used the same motherly tone as the one with which she used to tell her baby sister to come back to her after a nightmare. Briony would probably have understood.

4. Atonement attempts

4.1. Briony

In the beginning of the novel, Briony is a thirteen-year-old girl that the reader learns to know as a self-absorbed preadolescent. She likes to write, her creations being a medley of her childhood readings. She likes to use complicated words and likes their effect on her readers and, as here in the case of the play, on her future spectators. Briony sees the others as a means to make herself shine and acknowledges that she understands the secrets of everybody's minds.

This is how, in Part One, she has enough confidence to judge the scene happening by the fountain between Robbie and Cecilia. Any other child would be surprised or puzzled, but would later forget the scene because it could be interpreted as some sort of game or because it is too complicated to be understood without having heard anything. But Briony's fantasy needs less than that to be turned on: she has an explanation. What she saw must be the evidence of a certain kind of malefic power that Robbie has on Cecilia. Briony was longing for something exciting to happen in her life, "None of this was particularly an affliction; or rather, it appeared so only in retrospect, once solution had been found" (McEwan 5), and the fountain scene is just the beginning of it: Robbie, who she used to consider as familiar, now becomes suspicious. He is threatening Cecilia, and Briony, in her search for glory, thinks that she ought to protect her elder sister: from now on, she will keep an eye on her.

The day of the "rape" is a very particular day. Briony is forced to accept the fact that her play will not take place, and for the first time of her life, she has a real secret, "no one knew about the squirrel's skull beneath her bed, but no one wanted to know" (McEwan 5), and has the choice whether to keep it or to tell it. To evaluate Briony's atonement attempt, we have to wonder whether she was lying as she testified against Robbie, and if she did lie, what were the reasons that pushed her to do it.

4.1.1.   Briony's perception of the events on the day of the "rape"

> 'Do you think I assaulted your cousin?'
> 'Did you think it then?'
> She fumbled her words. 'Yes, yes and no. I wasn't certain.'
> 'And what's made you so certain now?'
> She hesitated, conscious that in answering she would be offering a
> form of defence, a rationale, and that it might enrage him further.
> 'Growing up.' (McEwan 342)

Briony answers Robbie that growing up helped her to understand that he was not guilty. Was she really as naive as she pretends?
Briony is actually an intelligent person. As a child, she already has talent for writing stories and understands the concept of order. Dreams and fantasies have a larger place in a child's mind that in the one of an adult and although Briony is fascinated by the adult world, she is not armed yet to penetrate its terrible secrets.

Briony opened the note that Robbie gave her for Cecilia by curiosity, but also because she thought that she might find an explanation of what she saw through her window in the morning. At that time, she did not know nor even suspect that Cecilia and Robbie were in love. The two themselves were in the process of putting words on what they felt. Briony has a very simple idea of love. According to her, it is a feeling that has its climax in the wedding ceremony ... and nothing after: "[...] her heroines and heroes reached their innocent climaxes and needed to go no further". Being a thirteen-year-old girl in the beginning of the twentieth century, and being Briony, she does not have a faintest clue about sexual intercourse and interprets everything that has to do with sensuality as bizarre . Anything that is too anatomical is obscene for her: "No one in her presence had ever referred to the existence of that part of her to which – Briony was certain – the word referred". Lola made good use of Briony's ignorance: the little girl could never have imagined that Lola's bruised arm was in fact not the result of an attack by the twins.

Briony lied as she testified against Robbie. She definitely knew that he was not the man that she saw "attacking" Lola. As she totally ignores what the sexual needs of two people attracted by each other are, the two brutal situations – for an innocent child, yes they are – she is confronted with, within a few hours, are perceived as aggression scenes. At the moment where she testifies, Briony is only sure of one thing: Robbie represents some kind of danger and must be removed from the Tallis household. She will be the one who will contribute to his eviction. Even if Cecilia does not yet understand that she is in danger, she will know it later – at the moment she is still under the power of Robbie and might have been seduced by the word that should not be pronounced in a civilized conversation and now probably sounded in her mind s well as it does in Briony's mind. She does not have in mind that he will spend many years in prison, nor that the criminal might be someone else: for her, he is just a devil and this certainty takes over the good sense and all her senses in general.
On the day of the "rape", Briony saw Paul Marshall, but her mind was so busy with the thinking of Robbie being a maniac, that it blinded her.

4.1.2.   Was the accusation a revenge?

The reader learns in the novel from Briony and from Robbie separately, but both after the "rape", that Briony once had a crush on Robbie: "[...] a real crush that had lasted days. Then she confessed it to him one morning in the garden and immediately forgot about it." (McEwan 342) This information could be interpreted as a clue from Mc Ewan as to the reason that pushed Briony to testify against Robbie. As he wanders through the war landscape in France, Robbie remembers the incident of the river and comes to the conclusion that Briony testified against him because she had been hurt by his reaction when she told him that she loved him. She had just dived into the water in order to check whether Robbie would save her or not. After he rescued her, she told him that she loved him. The only effect of this declaration after such an irresponsible act was to annoy Robbie even more. He probably wondered where were the limits of Briony's silliness.

Admitting that Briony denounced Robbie to revenge would mean to believe that she is able to love and that she is a person who holds grudges.

Briony stands for a very particular conception of love throughout the novel and also in the film. She has a very romantic, not to say naive, conception of love. Briony really loves Cecilia, or at least wants to give her back the affection she received from her, she only does not know how and is therefore destructive. Cecilia used to cuddle with the baby of the family and to comfort her after a nightmare.

For Briony, love is essentially platonic. Carnal love is irrelevant, and she only sees love through the attention or admiration it can draw on her own person. We see this as she names her husband, in Part Three, as if he were a part of the decoration. Nothing is told about his appearance, character or how and when she met him, when and why he died. Briony spends more time describing the process of choosing a dress for a later entrance, than to talk about her husband. The fact that Briony refuses up to her last days to use make up, make up meaning an attempt to be physically attractive, testifies again of this vision she has of love. We can suppose that as Briony represents self-love throughout the novel, she does not feel the need to be attractive to other people, as she means enough to herself. She finds satisfaction not in the men's desire but in the admiration people show her, men, women or children. Such a person, incapable of really loving someone, cannot be seriously harmed by Robbie's indifference. As she tells her mate while working in the hospital, the feeling disappeared as soon as she uttered the sentence.

Therefore the hypothesis of Briony wanting to revenge is not justified. Her accusation was really the one of an ignorant young girl possessed by her fantasies.

4.1.3.   Briony's "atonement"

Briony's self-absorption and ignorance altered her perception of the events of a day which would dramatically change the lives of Robbie, Cecilia, Paul, Lola and herself.

As she grows older, she dedramatizes what happened on the day of the "rape" and realizes that she was simply too immature to understand what was going on and who really acted badly. She accepts the fact that she is also guilty of a crime: contributing to the separation of two lovers. Although she is not able to empathize with Robbie and Cecilia, her atonement will consist in trying to offer them the happy moments they never had.

Briony's biggest sin, after testifying against Robbie, was her passivity. How many opportunities did she have to rectify her mistake? She could have called the police and changed her account of the events, she witnessed Paul and Lola's wedding and did not say a word. Briony is a profoundly weak person and that is probably one of the most annoying traits of her personality. The act of writing is the only thing and the best that she is able to do to make amends.

Writing is sometimes an efficient way to evade, to run away from the everyday life, but also a way to get rid of some uncomfortable feelings.

A diary is very often the only confident when one has to bear something he cannot tell nor write to anyone else.

We have seen earlier that one needs to put pride aside and be humble in order to atone. Briony's problem is that although she feels sorry for others in way, she cannot really understand how the situation looks from their perspective. She is still at the very beginning of that process.

Briony's cowardice will even go up to the fact of not even considering the publication of her novel before Paul and Lola's death: "I might outlive Paul Marshall, but Lola would certainly outlive me. The consequences of this are clear. The issue has been with us for years. As my editor put it once, publication equals litigation." (McEwan 359) Yet litigation is a small inconvenience compared to the death Robbie had or dying in the bombing of a tube station, as Cecilia did. "The pen is mightier than the sword" (Bulwer Lytton 308), but only if the holder of this pen means to use it as a weapon. After Briony's reflexion on the words of her editor, the reader is bound to wonder whether she wrote this novel only to have a hobby or if she actually planned to publish the novel at all. Publishing it right now would be the most courageous thing that Briony would ever have done, even now, so late, so much time after the events, even if Robbie and Cecilia died so long ago. The Marshalls might protest the content of the novel, but the controversy itself is more than enough to raise people's attention and let them come to their own conclusions. Moreover, it would be the best way to offer Robbie and Cecilia a haven of peace in the collective memory.

The truth is that Briony never had the faintest illusion the effect of her atonement attempt. How could she when she is not even able to face Lola and Paul Marshall, even so many years after the events? "No atonement for God, or novelists, even if they are atheists. It was always an impossible task, and that was precisely the point. The attempt was all." (McEwan 371)

Realizing what she has done to Cecilia and Robbie is the torment of her life; it haunts her wherever she goes, and is one of the key reasons that she releases the truth in novel form before she dies. She seeks some sort of atonement for her tragic mistake. But at the same time, Briony is only running away from the problem. If she had ever wished to do something to repair the damage she had caused, she had enough time and opportunities. In her case, the feeling of guilt is not strong enough to take a step and atone.

4.2. Robbie

Robbie's mistake on the day of the "rape" was to put the wrong version of his love letter to Cecilia in the envelope. He would bitterly regret it, as well as the moments spent with Cecilia in the library. Although he hated Briony for testifying against him, he also acknowledged that all this would never have happened if he and Cecilia had waited a bit or if he did not go alone as the search for the twins began.

Robbie's only fault was to be too confident in his future. He assumed that all his plans would one day come true, and strengthened by this thought and by his growing love for Cecilia, he was not afraid of anything.

Robbie feels guilty for not having waited more, for making love to Cecilia in the library. He is ashamed of being considered as a child molester. Serving as a soldier in France is for him a tragedy, an unfair punishment, but also a way to grow up, to discover that he is not the owner of his life, that other factors come into play... and also that there are greater afflictions than his own.
Robbie's atonement is more complete than Briony's because it is sincere and goes through physical challenges. He empathizes with his brothers of arms and the war victims, he is wounded, suffers mentally because of the graphic details of the situation and his memories of Cecilia. The hypothetical future meeting with her would be the reward for so many years of tribulations.

4.3.   Paul and Lola

Paul and Lola are the two real criminal figures in this novel. They are the two characters with fundamentally malign intentions.
Lola is not the innocent girl that she pretends to be. From the beginning of Part One on, where she interacts with the other children, the reader becomes aware of the fact that she plays a role and knows exactly when to pretend to be a victim to obtain what she wants. A good example is the way she literally steals Arabella's role from Briony. She plays on the fact that she has not enjoyed anything for months and suggests that she should therefore be pitied.
In the film, the way Lola looks at Danny Hardman as he enters the room to attend the rehearsal is more than evocative. It is the glance of a woman to a man, she finds him attractive.
Afterwards, Lola deliberately lies to Briony and tells her that the twins are the ones who gave her Chinese burns. She might have come to Briony with the desire to confess, but she then decided to hold on to her story. The reader too cannot know at this very moment that she is lying but this fact will become clearer during dinner, as Paul will wait for the absence of the twins to tell the supposed events of that afternoon. The climax of Lola's culpability is her lie by omission. By leaving Briony the freedom to designate the "rapist", she deliberately commits a crime and protects her shameful relationship with Marshall.

Paul Marshall is by far the most disgusting character in the novel. He comes into the Tallis household as a predator. Cecilia does not mind him. His pervert aspect appears to us as he dreams of his sisters standing around his bed, touching him and pulling his clothes. He then heads to the room where Lola and her brothers are. He observes them, especially Lola   who reminds him of Pre-Raphaelite paintings, portraying strange natural beauties, but also famous for the fascination they cause, namely due to their luxuriant loose hair. The thought that Marshall can compare these women to a child Lola might already has an idea of the effect she has on him as she plays the game and licks the chocolate before biting it as he tells her to do. There's a clear physical attraction between these two characters. We would rather talk about blossoming physical attraction between Lola and Marshall, than about love. He sees in her the woman she would like to be and she sees him as the important man he wants to be seen as.

Paul probably used Lola's naivety – she thought that she was already a woman – to his own benefit. Lola initiated and enjoyed the game of desire, turned him on, but did not necessarily have experience about its consequences and the sexual intercourse it was bound to provoke. After it happened, she was surprised by its brutality but enjoyed it. It is because she aspired to doing it again and could not face the shame that she would have to if the Tallis household discovered what was going on between her and Marshall that she decided to let them believe that Robbie was the "rapist". Lola played her part very well, whipping and keeping silent like the authentic victim of a rape. This way she also left Paul Marshall above any suspicion.

Paul and Lola are absolutely aware of the wrong they did, but it was for their own sake. They might have thought about it once or twice during all the years after that evening. Lola especially as she saw Briony at her wedding ceremony:

> Briony simply stared. All she wanted was for Lola to know she was there and to wonder why. The sunlight made it harder for Briony to see, but for a fraction of a moment, a tiny frown of displeasure may have registered in the bride's face. Then she pursed her lips and looked to the front, and then she was gone. (McEwan 326)

If they had any feeling of guilt, they tried to get rid of it by multiple donations. Nobody, except for Briony, would ever doubt the evidence that they are righteous people.

> They still appear in the newspapers occasionally, in connection with their Foundation and all its good work for medical research, or the collection they've donated to the Tate, or their generous funding of agricultural projects in sub-Saharan Africa. (McEwan 356)

5. Transferring the concepts of guilt and atonement to the film

After watching the film, most of the spectators are left very annoyed about Briony. She is held responsible for everything and it is hard to understand how someone can be so silly. This results from the fact that Briony has a much longer presence on the screen than the other characters, although they all share a part of guilt.

5.1.   Treatment of Briony's character

Briony is there so often on the screen because the novel is told by her.
The three actresses chosen to play Briony's part are blonde. As Joe Wright had enough money – *Atonement*'s budget was £15 million - to

afford choosing three brown-haired actresses, just as in the novel, it must have been a deliberate choice.

The director might have wished to accentuate the differences between Briony and Cecilia by making them physical. The cliché of an innocent or better person is often of a blonde one. This can be seen in commercials, for example, where the blonde woman always gives advice to the brown-haired one.

Briony in the film looks just as insignificant and elusive as in the novel. Thinking that she still could be up to such a great damage makes her annoying. Nevertheless, a spectator watching the film attentively should see that Briony cannot be held responsible for everything: in a trial, to be condemned severely, the suspect has to be held as fully aware of his actions. That's just not Briony's case, as we have seen in the previous chapters, she cannot really get a grip on the reality of life.

The only moments were she seems to be alive are the ones when she is working in the hospital: she touches, helps, cleans, exists.

5.2.   Treatment of Cecilia and Robbie's characters

In the first part of the film, when Danny Hardman waits in the living room for instructions as to where he should put Paul Marshall's luggage, Cecilia addresses him in a very scornful way, with the same superior tone as Briony later on during the rehearsal of the play. It is a clue from the director to indicate that Cecilia is not only a nice person.

In her relationship with Briony, she is protective, motherly, never violent, even after the tragic events leading to Robbie's incarceration. Nothing in her behavior nor her actions is really reprehensible. Her only fault was not to explain Briony what was going on as she had a chance to, i.e. after having been interrupted in the library, both hers and Robbie's fault.

The spectator can see how the time spent in prison, the war and the regrets changed Robbie. He is not the joyous young man from the beginning of the movie anymore. He is embittered, tormented.

5.3.   Treatment of Paul and Lola's characters

Lola Quincey and Paul Marshall have relatively short appearances on the screen: Lola in the beginning as a slightly older child aware of her power over the younger ones and clever in the art of using it; later as the flirting adolescent, the bruised victim of her two brothers, the victim of a rape, Marshall's fiancée and finally as a bride. Paul looks off-topic in any situation (Cecilia even qualifies him of being an idiot).

The spectator forgets both of them very fast and rejects all the fault for Cecilia and Robbie's separation on Briony's shoulders.

A film cannot last five hours only in order to retransmit each single detail of the novel. But it would have been clever from the director to include Marshall's dream about his sisters before his meeting with Lola: an excellent way to point out Paul's wicked aspect, together with the way he commanded Lola to bite his Amo chocolate.

6. Conclusion

Ian McEwan's *Atonement* is not only the story of a tormented woman desiring to make amends for a past mistake. It is a novel portraying the mechanisms of guilt and the need to atone.

Guilt is not necessarily a natural feeling. Everyone was born with a little bit of it and later becomes more or less sensitive to it, according to the received education and other experiences. The characters in the novel suffer from the disillusion not to be able to control their future though, paradoxically, a single mistake *they* did is in fact the cause of their disenchantment.

Cecilia and Robbie are essentially the victims of a crime. In a war context it would be exaggerated to pretend that, had Briony's, Paul's and Lola's behavior been different, Robbie and Cecilia would certainly have fulfilled their love. But their chances would have certainly been better.

The religious aspect of the term atonement has been completely forgotten in the film. There is no reference to God, apart from the wedding in the cathedral, which induces that – just like for the war - God witnesses injustice and remains silent. This omission has one plausible reason: in the novel, there is no God, Briony is God. She discovered the discomfort of feeling guilty throughout the years but still wants to escape any judgment. Her atonement was only an attempt and her novel will be published posthumously.

The themes of guilt and atonement disputed in the novel are definitely present in the film, but relegated to the second plan by the general impression of powerlessness. The characters are only pawns in a chess game, in Briony's chess game. As she confesses that a part of the story did not happen as she told it, we are divided between believing her and wondering whether she told anything true at all.

To conclude, we will acknowledge that the novel and the film support the idea that guilt without atonement is pointless, that intentions without actions are inefficient. *Atonement* is a strong statement against cowardice in its numerous forms.

7. Bibliography

- Simon, Ulrich. *Atonement: from holocaust to paradise.* Cambridge: James Clarke, 1987.
- Pruyser, Paul W, H. Newton Malony, Bernard Spilka. *Religion in Psychodynamic Perspective: The Contributions of Paul W. Pruyser.* Oxford: Oxford University Press, 1991.
- Prindle, William D. *21ˢᵗ Century King James Bible.* Iowa Falls: World Bible Publishers, Inc. , 1994
- Watson-Smyth, Kate. "Sean, 12, is the youngest father" *The Independent.* Independent News and Media Limited. 21 January 1998. independent.co.uk. http://www.independent.co.uk/news/sean-12-is-the-youngest-father-1139875.html
- *The Torah: The Five Books of Moses.* Philadelphia: Jewish Publication Society of America, 2000.
- McEwan, Ian. *Atonement.* London: Vintage Books, 2001.
- Watts, Fraser N., Rebecca Nye, Sara B. Savage. *Psychology for Christian ministry.* New York: Routledge, 2001.
- Ferrini, Paul. *Forbidden Fruit: Unraveling the Mysteries of Sin, Guilt and Atonement.* Greenfield: Heartways Press, 2002.
- Carr, Allan. *Positive Psychology: The Science of Happiness and Human Strengths.* New York: Routledge, 2003.
- *Atonement.* Joe Wright, Working Title. Digital Videodisc. Universal, 2008
- Sacks, Jonathan. "The Sin Offering". *Covenant and Conversation.* 28 March 2009: 1-4. http://www.chiefrabbi.org/UploadedFiles/Articals/vayikra5769.pdf
- Bulwer Lytton, Edward. *Richelieu: or, The conspiracy. A play in five acts, to which are added, Historical odes on the last.* Charleston : BiblioBazaar, 2009.
- Tierney, John. "Findings – Guilt and Atonement on the Path to Adulthood". *The New York Times.* 24 August 2009. The New York Times Company. http://www.nytimes.com/2009/08/25/science/25tier.html

YOUR KNOWLEDGE HAS VALUE

- We will publish your bachelor's and
  master's thesis, essays and papers

- Your own eBook and book -
  sold worldwide in all relevant shops

- Earn money with each sale

Upload your text at www.GRIN.com
and publish for free